Her Durian

Fida Islaih

Her Durian
Fida Islaih

Copyright by Fida Islaih 2019

Cover Design 2019 by Heather McCorkle

The Her Series

Her Olives
Her Treasures
Her Durian

For my grandmother and mother.

To my uncle Saif for joking about the title idea, "why I don't like durian."

Thank you to all my uncles and aunts for always teasing me that each new experience I had in Malaysia was a poem idea.

Table of Contents

Jungle

Malay Culture

The Dishes

Part 1

Travel

Plane Ride

On the plane
from home to home
I traded apples for coconuts
prairies for mountains

Going from where I stand out and explain
myself
about the headscarf and everything I do
to blending in with my headscarf
and not being asked about everything,
I am in wonder of the differences.

Ocean

Oceans between us
but our familial bond
keeps us together

I am waiting for the ocean
to wash away my tears
and to come into view
letting me know
I'm flying closer to my family

I am waiting for the ocean
to remind me to smile and laugh
not caring about the time

I'm waiting for the ocean
to let me create memories,
heal my heart and wake up my soul.

Car Ride

Excitement in the car ride
I try to listen
treated with orange juice
for being sick on the plane
stopping halfway so that they can pray

The heat is strong
but I'm happy
not letting it bother me
I fall asleep on the drive

After the reunion
with loud noises around me
I fall into an exhausted sleep
woken up to go to another house for the
night.

Our Arrival

You hold my hand
as we hear a unison of excited voices
the family all wait together
there is a blur of arms
as we hug each other
showering them with gifts
eating food that we missed
in the background of falling twinkle lights

The young cousins remember us
smiles never leaving their faces
we play around and almost don't notice
how we speak and they understand
we figure it out
they tried to learn our language
so that they can speak to us
when we're here.

Transportation

My first time on a plane
was on my way to Malaysia
I was young and don't remember it
but being on a plane
makes me anxious and claustrophobic
getting off I feel disoriented
the vacation and seeing family is worth it

My first time on a boat
was going to an island in Malaysia
it was fast and tipped to the side
I thought I would fall
but I loved the breeze and mist

My first time on a train was in Malaysia
knots in my stomach
I felt restless
they tried to talk to me and the distraction
helped
but it switched to what was about to
happen
how I felt and if I was happy
I couldn't speak
if I spoke, everything would spill
the shakiness and tears
I tried to breathe

The train felt cold and stuffy
I loved seeing the views of mountains
we passed by
and it rocked me to sleep.

Airports

Being at the airport
it feels familiar,
odd to have it memorized

Airports are the in between places
for creating memories
waiting for the adventure to start,
to see you again

My grandmother cries when she sees us
the sight makes me teary eyed
as we embrace each other
it's happy tears
of finally being here

Airports are bittersweet with hellos and
goodbyes
trying not to cry as we say goodbye
it's really see you later.

Travel Back

When I travel back home
I stay in the village
it's simpler there
they are not in rush
taking everything slowly
I had to adjust and I can tolerate it

The heat is so strong
There is patience for everything else
I don't like bugs but I can tolerate them

I adapt to their way of life
sitting on the floor with family
I learn to eat with my hands
eating rice from banana leaves
walking around the market
trying all the fruits and desserts
making a bowl of ais kacang

There is more meaning
in this trip I'm taking
than the life I live away from them.

Part 2

Family

Remember Their Faces

On our first day
there were fireworks to welcome us
but really there to celebrate Eid
it feels like it as we give out gifts
it was all a blur
but I will always remember their faces

Long car rides
with the same song on repeat
seeing the same sights
I saw years ago
it feels new and familiar at the same time
it was all a blur
but I will always remember their faces

The cool tiles under my feet
as I walk into their homes
we eat on the floor
swatting flies away
I tried to understand the language
but it was all a blur
I will always remember their faces

We gather together
it's chaotic as we play games
laughing at how we look

as we try to win our prizes
it happened so fast it's a blur
but I will always remember their faces.

They once gathered around me
as I told a story as a toddler
it feels like deja vu
as they gather around me
wanting to read the stories I've written
my face is flushed red
but I will always remember their faces

Getting ready together
waiting for the ceremony to start
learning of their traditions
my smile is so big
I will always remember their faces

The time has come to an end
I try not to think of it
as we talk of life
but a single word about leaving
and we are all in tears
hugs are shared
I will remember the smiles
will always remember their faces.

Day in Malaysia

The skittering of a lizard on the wall
opposite from where I sleep
I notice the shadow
as my eyelids close

The clucking of a chicken
wakes me up
heading downstairs
to the smells of spices
and the chatter of family

The heat welcomes me
as I embrace it,
both the weather and the food
swatting the flies
every morning my grandmother comes to
visit
sometimes we have unexpected guests
listening to the athan on the streets

The dark clouds loom
it starts to rain
lightly first and then heavy
with its big raindrops
the sound is a lullaby
watching from the open door

it calls us outside
we dance in the rain
as it cools the earth
the rain is different in Malaysia

this is my second home
and I have to say goodbye
until another year calls me back.

Meal Time

All my aunts
sit together on the floor
cleaning anchovies
a stray cat begs for scraps
eventually falling asleep at their feet

Family dinners feel like feasts
with so many aunts, uncles, cousins
it feels like thanksgiving day in the US
feels like Iftar with my friends in the US

it's joyous chaos
as we get our food and wait for more
wait for each other
trying to find a seat at the table
some of us sharing a chair or plate
but this is family in Malaysia.

Family Day

Butterflies danced around us
as we reunited,
taking family photos;

throwing flour at each other
after finishing the scavenger hunt,
being treated with ice cream

watching the water fall is calming
hearing laughter in the background

My uncles find durian to cut open
as we swat flies from our sticky fingers

I'm happy seeing everyone have fun
everyone playing in different groups
laughing with them, pausing to take it all in
I'm floating in between each of them

It was about to start raining
and she prayed that it won't
the sun came back out

Laughter echoes off the cool tiles
playing games and talking through the night
ending it with sparklers and fireworks
hearts warmed by love.

Dragonfly

Getting chased by a dragonfly
that my uncle caught
I didn't give it a single thought
all I could do was giggle
and wriggle -
away as I remembered a memory
my mother shared
of playing with dragonflies.

Opah's Kitchen

In my grandmother's kitchen
looking out to a jungle
and the clothes line

I enjoy eating the fruits
and swat at the flies
the smell of spices fill the room
as I watch my mom
and aunts help cook rice
and fold banana leaves

yet the kitchen table gives me anxiety
crowded with supplies and ingredients,
snacks and unnecessary things,
it's unorganized,
I watch my aunts and leave the room

I'll forget about the heat
as I look back on this memory.

Grandfather's Grave

We smell jasmine flowers
while visiting my grandfather's grave
reading Quran on him
and sending a prayer
it breaks my heart that I barely knew him
that it took so long to finally visit
throwing tiny flowers on his grave
May Allah have mercy on his soul.

Wedding

The family walks between both villages
giving their love to each other
rice is thrown at them
for good luck

Family gather together
as we start the ceremony

I can't focus on the camera
but I still smile
I don't remember taking the picture
but I love the people in it
and the memories surrounding it

An egg is given to each guest
for fertility for the newlyweds.

Song

The songs play
and I'm the only one swaying to the beat
in a room of people
to celebrate the union of two
I look around but I don't feel embarrassed
every culture is different
I'm sitting among family
who know me and won't judge
but I wonder if there is someone else at
another table
swaying to the beat.

Gifts

You came to visit
and I sat by you
watching what you were doing
you gave me a yellow scarf

The cold weather was new to you
I let you borrow my yellow sweater

I came along
and you passed the dress to me
but before that,
put your own touch
You added threads of sparkle
to the sleeves and hem of the dress
to make it look new.

Beach Breeze

The weather is hot
but there are pockets of coolness
with the beach breeze,
we walk on the beach each morning
watching the tide
I love the sound of the waves
the waves are big
letting them wash over me

we lay on the beach all day
only getting up to move our seats
and walk to town for lunch
sweating in the heat
our skin gets kissed by the sun
our feet kissed by mosquitoes

we walk to the market each night
getting dinner and souvenirs
Listening to the waves
as I wake up and go to sleep.

Visit Malaysia

The last country I visited was Malaysia
with views of mountains
I'm appreciated
for speaking the native language
I learn to navigate the streets
the markets filled with
food, clothes and handmade goods
I come back with friends asking how it was
and that they want to visit Malaysia.

Raya

The streets are decorated for Raya
Raya is all about a caravan of people
going house to house
eating a variety of food, fruits and desserts
little cookies in cute jars
for guests to enjoy
consistently making food and cleaning in
between

giving salaams to aunts and uncles
for eid money
standing in the heat
to take pictures of the family
in their baju Raya
color coordinate our outfits
looking for the perfect views
of the mountains and the kampung.

Thailand

Family is for traveling together
by train we went to Thailand
where women powder their faces white,
vendors try to get you to buy from them
shopping and sitting together
we get to bond
finally feeling close

Cats sit by me while I eat
my aunts and uncles
share food with each other
keep feeding me
telling me to try everything
it's an experience
saying I'm full means nothing to them

It's a long day of eating and shopping
we do some sightseeing
a monkey pulls on my pants
and two follow me for food

We have a crazy tuktuk ride
at every stop we fall on each other
all we can do is laugh and pray
thank God we all made it in one piece
as we look forward

to traveling more together.

Travel

I want to travel the world
have experiences and make memories
but my heart misses home

A sense of relief
when I arrive at my uncle's house
comfortable in my own space
instead of on edge about my surroundings.

Jungle

Driving deep into the jungle
got an armful of durian
from the trees my grandfather planted
we find a gem
a river flows through
with its small waterfall
big rocks scattered to sit on
and enjoy the view
and the sound of water
toes in the sand
made wudu in the river
before leaving the calm.

Part 3

Malay Culture

Cultural Influence

Malaysia is a fusion of cultural influence
indigenous people, Chinese and Indian,
try the different dishes
with the burst of flavor and richness of
taste

some Arabic words made it into the Malay
language
Malay used to be written with Arabic letters

and look at the architecture
the mosques, churches and temples
built with touches of Chinese or Arab.

Adapt to Culture

I'm Arab by my looks
and Malay by my attitude
American Muslim by lifestyle
I try to blend into both

learning the language
loving the food

culture of the place matters
work on understanding
and adapting to the social setting

I wear a bright caftan in Malaysia
but in America I'll look out of place

learn to cut open a coconut
eat a piece of durian
learn to eat with our hands

my family watches me
surprised by how well
I am able to adapt.

Affection

I come from a country
where I see
public displays of affection
all around me
being here is a shock
not seeing any
public displays of affection

My parents hold hands
and my grandmother says
it'll break their wudu

My sister wears the headscarf
and my aunt adjusts the scarf
to cover the tiny bit of exposed skin

I hold my mom's hand
while on the streets
for our safety

My grandmother lays her hand on me
as we listen to the chatter around us
I appreciate her presence

I can still see the love
sharing a plate of food
drink from the same cup

a kiss and salaam
on the back of his hand.

Barriers

There are several barriers to break
language, age, gender
I speak fast and they don't understand
it's hard to bond with my younger cousins
I'm not social
and I don't know what they are into
I have to find my way around

There are several barriers to break
culture and religiosity
feeling like I'm being judged
I'm learning a new side
and trying to adapt
balancing how to be
in different communities

There are several barriers to break
an arab girl tries tempoyak with salmon
mixing durian with the mung bean dessert
eating durian itself
there are fermented foods
and foods with shrimp paste
eating fish from its bones
I'm adventurous
truly Malay.

Language Barrier

The language barrier may be hard
but we recognize the love
we have for each other
sitting together
looking through photos
letting you feed me

The next time I come around,
similar to my cousins,
my grandmother tries to speak
a few words in English
and I will try the same.

Salaam After Prayer

Sitting with my Muslim American sisters
during Eid prayer, after the khutbah
we say salaam, embracing each other
for making it through fasting
and celebrating this joyous day

Coming to Malaysia
I notice a different ritual
after each prayer I kiss my grandmother
and aunts' hand
giving salaam to those we prayed with
showing our love for each other
for the sake of God

Across the world
we all show up for God together
listening to his words
praying to ease our hearts.

Missing Something

Being in Malaysia
it feels like I'm missing something
is this what being homesick feels like?
it feels like my life back home is on pause

I spent most of Ramadan in America
late night drives of going to the masjid
feels like I am the only one awake
It's something special and holy
between me and God
taking the month to complete the Quran
during taraweeh

I'm missing the Muslim American style Eid
of walking into a big gym
with takbeerat in the background
seeing our whole community gather
together to pray
staying afterwards for games and
conversations
treats and photographs
taking a break at home before continuing
the festivities

Despite it
I'm grateful for my experience in Malaysia

it's starting to feel like another home.

Call Her Aunt

I call the women around me
my aunts and sisters
it is a sign of respect and travels across
from my Arab American side to my Malay
side
my cousins call me kak
and I call my aunts makcik
yet I simply call my mom mama

but it wasn't always like that
I never grew up around the Malay culture
like i did with the arab culture
coming to Malaysia
my cousins wonder why
I called my aunts and uncles by their first
names
still using Ammu for our uncles
they were disappointed

we gave it a try and it felt odd
anyways it was hard to remember and we
forgot
but I know the more I'm around the culture
I'll remember and adapt
they forgave us and let us do it our way.

Conversations

I may be working on understanding Malay
but I don't know how to speak Malay
I can only listen to a conversation
instead of being a part of it
I worry I may interpret what I heard wrong

but there are moments
when it's the two of us
we get a chance to bond
and I speak to you in English
I finally feel like I'm close to you.

Our Talks

Over lunch and midnight talks
everything from music and culture
to politics and anxiety
you see my happy side to my serious side

It's in my Arab genes
to talk with my hands
we are an expressive people
loud and intense

Malays are quiet and soft
patient with each other

two cultures are fighting in my heart
after a month of keeping quiet
I feel the urge to let out the louder side of
me

I hope you finally get the chance
to get to know me.

Part 4

The Dishes

Well Rounded Plate

Before leaving America
I enjoy all the Arab and American
dishes I can
I prep for Malaysia
and my mouth waters for the food

My mom makes Arab food
for her Malay family to try
enjoying the beach
we find Arab restaurants to try

I miss my friends in America
but I also miss the food
by the end of the trip
I crave for American style dishes
we get halal burgers that we usually can't
get
but I enjoy all the Malay dishes I can
before I go back and start missing them

Memories taste much sweeter
but the food is close
when it's made by loved ones.

Arab in Malaysia

Different is being transported
into Malaysian culture in the middle of an
American farm
it is enjoying Syrian food in Malaysia

Eating at an Arab restaurant in Malaysia
I'm asked if I speak Arabic
I'm shy and they are disappointed

Getting my nails done
the ladies said I look beautiful because I'm
Arab
I'm asked if I speak Malay
and they test my knowledge

you'll hear me switch
between three languages of English
and the little bit of Malay and Arabic I
know.

It's A Mix

Everything is so good
my mouth is on fire
the foods taste intense with the spiciness
dishes are a mix of salty and nutty flavors
with a hint of bitterness or sweetness

There are different kinds of meat dishes
but it's the sauces that make it unique
the fresh vegetables cool my tongue

Rojak is a salad
with fried tofu and cucur
savory or sweet, like ais kacang
the condiments are meant to be mixed
together.

Drowned in Milk Tea

Every morning
I would wake up
to a fresh cup of teh tarik

I knew it as milk tea
always seeing my mom pour it
back and forth between two cups
we ask why
but we were too young to understand
she said it was to make it cold faster

But teh tarik literally means pulled tea
a method to make it frothier.

Different Teas

The aroma of lychee is strong
like having the actual fruit
instead I'm having tea for breakfast

we visit the tea plantation
stocking up on the different flavors

The smell of lychee tea brewing
transports me back to my aunt's house
trying it for the first time

We have tea every night
It's the way my parents say I love you
asking me to make them tea
and saying it's the best

I want to enjoy tea time
with my loved ones
the tea is refreshing and soothing
like our conversations

This is something we should do together
sitting together means a lot to me.

Dessert

Dessert is supposed to be
something sweet
but tapai is sour
it's a sweet rice dessert

kek lapis is layered cake
in different flavors
a rainbow or coffee
sweet and sour

Another traditional dessert is pandan balls
filled with liquid palm sugar
and coated in grated coconut
a new favorite
with its chewiness and burst of sweetness.

Ais Kacang

Corn ice cream
Red bean ice cream
are the closest you can get
to ais kacang
i've been thinking of it
everyday since we left
until the day we arrived back

We eat it everyday
refreshing from the heat
shaved ice in rose syrup
topped with corn, peanuts,
beans and jellies.

Cendol

I've had many chances
to try it before
but I never have
until the first time this trip

Similar to ais kacang
shaved ice with jellies
it's a sweet dessert
with coconut milk and palm sugar.

Mango Sticky Rice

In Malay it's called
pulut mangga
a traditional Thai dessert
made with glutinous rice,
fresh mango and coconut milk,

Sweet mango
I have it several times
in our short trip to Thailand
my aunt orders it for me
and gets extra mango for me to enjoy
with a side of a lychee slushy

As I learned
you can substitute mango for durian
in the dessert with sticky rice
I haven't tried it but I know
durian is overwhelming
I can have only a few pieces
they say I sound like a local saying that.

Fruits

In the tropics
people who live there
are blessed to be there
with every kind of tree
fresh fruits and vegetables

my hands are sticky
with sweet juice from my favorite fruits
rambutan and mangosteen
the mangos here are actually sweet

juice is freshly blended
watermelon is my favorite
add lychee to it
I enjoy it everyday.

Front Porch

Sitting on the front porch
eating mangosteen
with my aunts and uncles
my hands sticky with juice
and stained red
mangosteen is the queen of fruits

Opening a durian
is hard work
I hope the fruit is worth it
you say the value of the fruit
is worth the work
durian is the king of fruit.

Her Rambutan

It's the first fruit I tried
years ago
on my first trip to Malaysia
there was a Rambutan tree
by my grandmother's house
it quickly became my favorite.

Coconut

Coconut falls from the tree
has many different uses
sweet juice to enjoy
meat of the fruit to eat as is
add it to drinks, dessert or a warm meal.

Dislike Durian

Why I don't like durian:
it's smelly and tastes rotten
the smell and taste never leaves

On the last day of our trip
they make us try it
I get the tiniest piece
and say I like it
they tease me that I still don't like it
not today but another time
I'll try a bigger piece.

Her Durian

I'm surrounded by the fruit
watching it drop from the tree
every market stall sells them

staying away from durian
not liking the smell
I get used to it
always being in the house

I finally try it
I have several pieces
each piece is different
It's fruit white or yellow
stringy and creamy
all sweet, some with a bit of bitterness
it's messy yet delicious to eat

they are all surprised that I love it
only getting the best for us.

Part 5

Multicultural

Uncover Culture

I used to dismiss my Malay culture
the Arab culture took over
one culture isn't better than the other
culture

it was in my surroundings every day
the language I hear
the food we cook and eat
and the people I spend time with

I didn't mean for that to happen
it broke my heart when I noticed it

There aren't many Malay around
eventually the community grows
and we make the time to be with them

those things are what make
my home and me unique
I've come to appreciate it

embracing it fully
I'm making up for the years missed
catching up on what I could've learned
feeling behind on what could've been
still proud to be a part of it.

An Arab Tries Malaysia

I had a moment of gratitude
when enjoying the dessert
for being Asian
without the food and culture
I would be missing out
I got lucky
two cultures in one

I'm an Arab American
they think I don't like fish
each time we eat
my uncle make sure to bring chicken
but I surprise them
and eat the fish
learning to clean it of the bones
and enjoy it more

Again, I tried something new
Apam balik with its fluffy pancake
filled with peanuts and cream corn
it reminds me of the nuts and raisins in
qatayif

With two cultures
I won't think of one or the other
I will always think of both

every mixed kid understands
making it my own
a new kind of culture.

Malay Mother

My Malay mother
making a Palestinian dessert
the house smells sweet
of vanilla, lemon and coconut
my Malay mother
wears a Palestinian thobe

I'm grateful two different people
embrace each other
people evolve
and culture should evolve too
if there isn't a culture
we will make our own.

Bilingual

It takes a lot of brain power
to familiarize and understand
a new language

I get the words
of the two different languages
(Arabic and Malay)
mixed up

I'm always asked if I can speak
the pressure around me
I say no
instead of testing my limited knowledge
afraid of how I'll sound
with the pronunciation and accent

I slowly pick up words
understand the context,
know the conversation

I know more than they realize
more than I realize
I have the courage to speak
and they smile proudly
when they hear me

without being fluent

my mouth is dry.

Mixed Views

A mixed person is looked down
upon in America
someone from the outside is left alone
I feel like I'm not enough to stand for them
and I don't belong

A mixed person is highly looked
upon in Malaysia
Malaysia is more open
to someone from the outside,
they accept them.

Mix of Cultures

I see a little boy with his mom
asking her for help
she wraps a long bright colored cloth
tied around his waist
to make a sarong
I don't feel like I'm here
but back in the country it's from

A little girl finds a headscarf
and asks her mom to put it on
she sees other women wear it
and wants to feel like she belongs

A woman walks into the mosque
and wants to respect the place
she asks for a headscarf

A young woman fidgets with her sari
another tries to wear the headscarf
but can't get it to stay properly
and asks for help

Being on the beach
is a different experience
in the west you see people in bikinis
but in the east you see people covered up

It's a time of celebration
the room is colorful
with everyone wearing
their different traditional dresses

America a place of many cultures
Desi, Malay and Arab
I take it all in.

It's A Cultural Thing

We eat on the floor
our family is big
I learned to eat with my hand
it's a cultural thing

Give salaam
with two or three kisses on the cheek
or kiss their hand
it's a cultural thing

I awkwardly stand out in my street clothes
wearing a sarong or telekung
during prayer
it's a cultural thing

Give salaam after prayer
and a kiss on the hand on Eid morning
it's a cultural thing

I'm learning to balance it all
as a I adapt to my different surroundings
of community and culture.

Malay Culture Raised Me

The Malay culture raised me
I wear brightly colored baju kurung
we communicate through food and
pictures

There is a language barrier
I teach my cousins English
as they teach me the Malay language
listening to my odd accent

The Malay culture raised me
on how to address
the different people in my family

The Malay culture raised me
I'm greeted with the smell
and sounds of Malaysia
I try new foods
fish and durian
fill the house
they watch the weird faces I make
the food and family
warm my heart.

They tease and remind me
of all the ideas for poetry

as my aunt translates a piece
I wrote to my grandmother

The Malay culture raised me
to be soft.

Birthday

Celebrating my birthday in Malaysia
with cake and durian
it's awkward and I feel shy
my family singing in multiple languages
my little cousin sings happy birthday
blowing out candles

I celebrate with my uncles
whose birthdays are close to mine
we say a little prayer for each other
before cake and cut it together

the family takes pictures
and I see them immediately
I take a few pictures too
I put my phone away and pause
I want to be present in my own celebration.

A Mixed Household

In Malaysia everything is quiet and slow
I come back to my American home
to my Palestinian cousins living with us
they fit in with the family
it's constantly loud
learning new dishes
and of each other's cultures

I wear the hijab everyday
trying to break out of my social anxiety shell
but I still need my quiet space

A Malay's main dish is fish and rice
while an Arab's main dish is meat and bread

an Arab overseas is different
from an Arab in America,
in Muslim America
it's about looking past borders
all the different Arabs come together
all the cultures are appreciated
introduced to foods from every country
instead of just the one you're from

They speak in Arabic to each other
my dad forgets and speaks Arabic to mama

I'm able to pick it up
understand words and conversations

Sometimes I glow
telling the differences
other times my heart dims
from the ignorance.

Part 6

Muslim American

Closed Doors & Open Scars

With being multicultural
I never felt like I was part of a community
we can't speak Arabic
so we can't be a part of the conversation
yet being in a muslim neighborhood was
the closest thing I had
to feeling like I was in a community

I always had a inkling
that a barrier was there
and with each step I see it
some people in this community
make it more known that it's there

We've been together for years
you broke the ties
closed the door and I have an open scar

Our friendship doesn't matter
I'm no longer part of our community
my heart hurts
I used to praise you and love you
it will take awhile for me to forgive you

I want to leave this place
and make my own community

with those I still love.

Mosque As A Second Home

A historical site
and place of worship
beautifully designed

The dome that shines on the horizon
the minaret where the prayer is called
soft mats to place our foreheads
standing shoulder to shoulder

Memories that should stay and live
this is my second home.

Muslim Responsibility

I grew up in a culture and community
where it's our responsibility
to visit the sick and the grieving
we receive enough food to feed a village
We remind each other
of finding strength in our faith in God.
It can be hard with our differences
and languages
but grieving moments like this
remind me how grateful I am for my
community.

Muslims of the World

Anxiety can take a back seat
as I enjoy the celebrations
I can't capture the excitement and pride,
there is so much happiness
I feel the vibration of the music and dance
new and experienced join the dabke circle
a dance from Palestine

I grew up around diversity
embracing and exploring cultures
and finding comfort in hearing different
languages

It's not about race but being human
the togetherness of going beyond borders
and connecting to our roots
remembering the origins
the blood in you

We make connections
accepting and elevating each other
never forget who you are
but don't let it hold you back from the
future.

International Phone Call

Saving up money
to make an international phone call
once a month
to our family
having a good conversation
it's hard to say bye
but we have to
I want to be there with them
a city I love and call home
I left to never stay but only visit
I will always carry the city in my heart
I'm happy here
where the opportunities are better,
in both places
the language barrier
and culture get in the way.

Cultural Traits

Being multicultural
the difference are at the forefront
it's the tangible things
like clothing and food

It's intangible things
like how we act
Malay's quiet patience
and Arab's loud intensity
I need space to be loud and expressive.

Foreign Language

The language sounded foreign
but started to feel familiar
I began to understand the words and
culture
smiling at knowing what they are saying

I started with Arabic
I love the meaning behind the words
the language is poetic, emphasizing the love
I try to speak but my accent is odd
I pick up the dialect
feeling comfortable in it
being raised in the culture helps

but as I pick up another language
hearing Malay
of the other half of me
it sounds and feels odd
I don't want to hear it
but I will learn the language
and pick it up comfortably
picking up the dialect and accent
I sound Malay

like I did with its culture and Arabic
learning to make both a part of me.

Salaam

The Arabic language has roots
defining the underlying meaning of
different words,
influencing other languages
one word can mean many things in
different languages

Salaam means peace in Arabic
used as a greeting among Arabs and
Muslims
Salamat means thank you in Tagalog
Selamat means safe in Malay
combined with expressions
hoping for goodness.

Part 6

Looking Back

Leaving

At the airport
I try not to be sad about leaving
they try to make me laugh
that a year is short and will come by fast

I remember how early we buy our tickets
and start planning
we promise to keep in touch
there are less tears than the last goodbye.

Six Months Later

Our days were packed with adventures
I don't remember taking the picture
but I love the people in it
and the memories surrounding it
you can feel the joy in our smile.

Picture

Pictures matter
especially the candid ones
they take you back to visualize
the experience and emotion
of the memories
instead of something blurry
in the back of your mind
through the pictures
you can feel the joy in our smiles.

Remember

I'm grateful for my two homes
one full of noise
the other quiet
but both filled with
love and laughter
heart to heart conversations

It took me awhile
to feel comfortable and open up
I felt empty and quiet
during my visit
like a shadow
until the end
with pockets of attention
I was part of the conversations

Home is always
the place that
unites us;
home is a place
unique to you.

Left Behind

We take off
the landscape gets smaller
a whole new view of a sunset
tiny lights twinkle
anticipating how it'll go

the coming brings excitement
as we get closer
and see the cityscape
with the mountains around it
I want to get there sooner
the time to move faster but then pause
it feels familiar and new at the same time

the leaving brings sadness
I feel like I left you behind
but a piece of you
is always with me
a part of me is everywhere.

Bracelets

He gifted her a set of gold bracelets
later she gave them to my mom
and eventually she hands them down to me

Every time I look down
at my wrists
and see the bracelets
I see their hands,
I am reminded of both women
who wore it before me
I hope to embody their strength.

Thank You

I hope you know how appreciative I am
thank you for letting us stay at your place
for driving us around town and feeding us
we are actually here
not just another photo you see.

Happiness

You can see it on my face
my eyes light up
my smile grows
as I enjoy the good things around me

My heart feels light
being around the world
filling it with laughter.

Bittersweet

Summer memories are bittersweet
I love being with my family
but knowing I have to say goodbye
until the time comes again
the year passes by fast
this trip feels a part of the last one
I hope the gap stays small
and the distance doesn't grow long.

Last Days

Counting down the days until we leave
making special requests
grateful that they can make it happen
I soak up the moments with you
trying to stay present
last moments with my favorite dishes
my heart is full of happiness and love.

Goodbyes

The countdown starts
there's a farewell dinner
when you talk
about us leaving
my walls break down
and it's easier for me to cry

the baby cousins fall asleep
I don't want to bother them
I kiss their cheeks and forehead
it hurts when I hear that after I left
they woke up asking about me

The most heartbreaking moment
of saying goodbye to family
is with my grandmother
never knowing if it's the last one.

I Love You

Loving you to the moon and back
is just an expression
the distance doesn't matter
I love you more than anything
more than I can imagine
add in all the other planets
fly to Mars
there is no way to measure love
I love you till Jannah.

Author Notes

1. The poem 'Malay Culture is also published in Rising Soul.

Glossary

Baju kurung - traditional Malay dress
Selamat hari raya - happy holidays
Tempoyak - a condiment made from fermented durian

Acknowledgments

Thank you to Heather McCorkle for the book cover. Thank you to Sarah Chafin and my mother for taking their time to read and give me feedback on my poems.

Thank you to my family and friends for their continued love and support.

About the Author

Fida Islaih is a self published poet of several collections. Islaih is also a poetry editor. You can find her on instagram @poetfida.

www.ingramcontent.com/pod-product-compliance
Lightning Source LLC
Chambersburg PA
CBHW031308130726
47988CB00007B/2767